God
PLEASE HELP ME FIND A
JOB
JOURNAL & JOB SEARCH ORGANIZER

SONIA H CAMERON

GOD, PLEASE HELP ME FIND A JOB: JOURNAL
AND JOB SEARCH ORGANIZER

Copyright © 2020 by Sonia H Cameron

ISBN: 978-1-7349724-3-6

All rights reserved. No part of this work may be reproduced or transmitted in any form or by any means without written permission from the publisher.

All scripture quotations are taken from
THE HOLY BIBLE

Scripture marked (NIV) NEW INTERNATIONAL VERSION
Scripture marked (KJV) KING JAMES VERSION
Scripture marked (NKJV) NEW KING JAMES VERSION
Scripture marked (GNT) GOOD NEWS TRANSLATION
Scripture marked (NLV) NEW LIVING TRANSLATION

I dedicate this book to all of the unemployed and underemployed individuals who are on the quest to find their dream job

Table Of Contents

Introduction 7

SECTION I: THE EMOTIONS OF THE JOBSEEKER. 9
    Fearful Job Seeker. 11
    Anxious Job Seeker 17
    Job Seeker with Low Self Esteem 23
    Job Seeker with Low Self Esteem 29
    Depressed Job Seeker. .35

SECTION II: THE STATUS OF THE JOB SEEKER 41
    Brand New Job Seeker .43
    Freelancer 49
    The Fired Job Seeker .55
    Long-time Job Seeker .61
    Temporary Employee Who Wants Full-time Employment 67
    Job Seeker with Financial Problems. 73
    When Jobs Are Scarce And Unemployment High 79

SECTION III: THE NEEDS OF THE JOB SEEKER 85
    Decision Making for Job Seekers 87
    Job Seeker Wanting To Relocate 93
    Changing Careers 99
    Job Seeker Working Remotely. 105
    Needing A Breakthrough. 111

SECTION IV: THE JOB SEARCH PROCESS 117
    Job Seeker Who Needs Connections 119
    Job Seeker's Resume 125
    Preparing For The Interview 131
    Job Offer. 137

    Giving Thanks For The Job 143
    Job Seeker Who Desires To Walk In Excellence. 149
Affirmations 154
Job Search Organizer 157
It's Not Over 201
About the Author. 203

Introduction

While writing *God, Please Help Me Find A Job*, I concluded that a job seeker would eventually find their own voice to pray for their specific needs. God customizes his guidance to each individual during the job search. Your career journey is as unique as your DNA. When you find your own voice, your prayers become more powerful. This book is a guide to creating your own prayers for your job search. It is a practical companion to the book God, Please Help Me Find A Job by Sonia H Cameron.

This book provides a framework for effective prayer. It starts with praise to God, then moves to confession of sins. After that is a petition for your desire or need. Finally give thanks for the blessing. Always ending in Jesus' Name. In addition to the prayer section, there are two sections for reflection on and testimony of what God has done.

In the middle of this book is a list of affirmations from the original book God, Please Help Me Find A Job. These affirmations allow you to state your truth in this season. By making a definite affirmation, you change your mindset to align with what God thinks of you and how He will perform miracles in your life.

This book also contains a job search organizer to assist you in keeping a record of your job search contacts and arrange your information in one space. The job search organizer details each encounter and each organization with which you connect. This is an essential tool to an effective and stress-free job search.

SECTION I

The Emotions
OF THE JOBSEEKER

When you lose your job, you start a grieving process. Initially, you might be upset or angry; however, eventually, you accept your loss and move on. Only God can bring peace during that season. Jesus spoke to the storm and the winds and waves became still. The same is true of the storms in life; you must talk to God to understand and navigate the storm.

Prayer Focus
FEARFUL JOB SEEKER

Scripture: Isaiah 41:13

Write the scripture: read it aloud.

Praise: Focus on one attribute of God and give Him Praise.

Confession: Tell a forgiving God about your sins and ask for His forgiveness.

Petition: Make your specific request known to God.

Thanksgiving: Give thanks after making your petition; the blessing is on the way. Praise God for the blessing you anticipate.

In Jesus' Name, Amen.

Write your own personal Prayer

Reflection: How has God blessed you before?

Testimony: How has God exceeded your expectations in the past?

SEEKING GOD...EVEN MORE

Read the prayer from the book again; then read the prayer you've written. As you consider the prayers and listen for God's divine help in your job search, what action can you take this week, based on what you are hearing from God?

PLAN YOUR CONVERSATION WITH GOD.

Create an environment for prayer and reflection...where will you pray... what will you surround yourself with?

Will you listen to music to get into his presence? Or will there be total silence?

Commit to a specific time in the morning or in the evening to connect with God for five minutes.

PLAN TO ACT AFTER HEARING FROM GOD.

Decide who you will connect to for help related to your job search; include former coworkers, friends, mentors and organizations you belong to. Write down the contact information and follow through.

Who? _____

Contact Info? _____

How? _____

When? _____

Results of Contact: _____

_____

_____

You are taking a step closer to your dream job.

Prayer Focus:
ANXIOUS JOB SEEKER

Scripture: Psalm 34:4

Write the scripture: read it aloud.

Praise: Focus on one attribute of God and give Him Praise:

Confession: Tell a forgiving God about your sins and ask for His forgiveness.

Petition: Make your specific request known to God .

Thanksgiving: Give thanks after making your petition; the blessing is on the way. Praise God for the blessing you anticipate.

In Jesus' Name, Amen.

Write your own personal Prayer

Reflection: How has God blessed you before?

Testimony: How has God exceeded your expectations in the past?

SEEKING GOD...EVEN MORE

Read the prayer from the book again; then read the prayer you've written. As you consider the prayers and listen for God's divine help in your job search, what action can you take this week, based on what you are hearing from God?

PLAN YOUR CONVERSATION WITH GOD.

Create an environment for prayer and reflection...where will you pray... what will you surround yourself with?

Will you listen to music to get into his presence? Or will there be total silence?

Commit to a specific time in the morning or in the evening to connect with God for five minutes.

PLAN TO ACT AFTER HEARING FROM GOD.

Decide who you will connect to for help related to your job search; include former coworkers, friends, mentors and organizations you belong to. Write down the contact information and follow through.

Who? _____

Contact Info? _____

How? _____

When? _____

Results of Contact: _____

_____

_____

You are taking a step closer to your dream job.

Prayer Focus

JOB SEEKER WITH LOW SELF ESTEEM

Scripture: 1 Peter 5:6-7

Write the scripture: read it aloud.

Praise: Focus on one attribute of God and give Him Praise:

Confession: Tell a forgiving God about your sins and ask for His forgiveness.

Petition: Make your specific request known to God.

Thanksgiving: Give thanks after making your petition; the blessing is on the way. Praise God for the blessing you anticipate.

In Jesus' Name, Amen.

Write your own personal Prayer

GOD, PLEASE HELP ME FIND A JOB

Reflection: How has God blessed you before?

Testimony: How has God exceeded your expectations in the past?

SEEKING GOD...EVEN MORE

Read the prayer from the book again; then read the prayer you've written. As you consider the prayers and listen for God's divine help in your job search, what action can you take this week, based on what you are hearing from God?

PLAN YOUR COMMUNICATION WITH GOD...

Create an environment for prayer and reflection...where will you pray...what will you surround yourself with?

Will you listen to music to get into his presence? Or will there be total silence?

Commit to a specific time in the morning or in the evening to connect with God for five minutes.

PLAN TO ACT AFTER HEARING FROM GOD.

Decide who you will connect to for help related to your job search; include former coworkers, friends, mentors and organizations you belong to. Write down the contact information and follow through.

Who? _____

Contact Info? _____

How? _____

When? _____

Results of Contact: _____

_____

_____

You are taking a step closer to your dream job.

Prayer Focus

JOB SEEKER WITH LOW SELF ESTEEM

Scripture: 1 Peter 5:6-7

Write the scripture: read it aloud.

Praise: Focus on one attribute of God and give Him Praise:

Confession: Tell a forgiving God about your sins and ask for His forgiveness.

Petition: Make your specific request known to God

Thanksgiving: Give thanks after making your petition; the blessing is on the way. Praise God for the blessing you anticipate.

In Jesus' Name, Amen.

Write your own personal Prayer

Reflection: How has God blessed you before?

Testimony: How has God exceeded your expectations in the past?

SEEKING GOD...EVEN MORE

Read the prayer from the book again; then read the prayer you've written. As you consider the prayers and listen for God's divine help in your job search, what action can you take this week, based on what you are hearing from God?

PLAN YOUR CONVERSATION WITH GOD.

Create an environment for prayer and reflection...where will you pray... what will you surround yourself with?

Will you listen to music to get into his presence? Or will there be total silence?

Commit to a specific time in the morning or in the evening to connect with God for five minutes..

PLAN TO ACT AFTER HEARING FROM GOD.

Decide who you will connect to for help related to your job search; include former coworkers, friends, mentors and organizations you belong to. Write down the contact information and follow through.

Who? _____

Contact Info? _____

How? _____

When? _____

Results of Contact: _____

_____

_____

You are taking a step closer to your dream job.

Prayer Focus:
DEPRESSED JOB SEEKER

Scripture: 2 Corinthians 1:3-4

Write the scripture: read it aloud.

Praise: Focus on one attribute of God and give Him Praise:

Confession: Tell a forgiving God about your sins and ask for His forgiveness.

Petition: Make your specific request known to God .

Thanksgiving: Give thanks after making your petition; the blessing is on the way. Praise God for the blessing you anticipate.

In Jesus' Name, Amen.

Write your own personal Prayer

Reflection: How has God blessed you before?

Testimony: How has God exceeded your expectations in the past?

SEEKING GOD...EVEN MORE

Read the prayer from the book again; then read the prayer you've written. As you consider the prayers and listen for God's divine help in your job search, what action can you take this week, based on what you are hearing from God?

PLAN YOUR CONVERSATION WITH GOD.

Create an environment for prayer and reflection...where will you pray... what will you surround yourself with?

Will you listen to music to get into his presence? Or will there be total silence?

Commit to a specific time in the morning or in the evening to connect with God for five minutes..

PLAN TO ACT AFTER HEARING FROM GOD.

Decide who you will connect to for help related to your job search; include former coworkers, friends, mentors and organizations you belong to. Write down the contact information and follow through.

Who? _____

Contact Info? _____

How? _____

When? _____

Results of Contact: _____

_____

_____

You are taking a step closer to your dream job.

SECTION II
THE STATUS OF THE JOB SEEKER

Your status determines your frame of mind. Believing that God will make your status temporary takes faith. Talking to God about your status gives you confidence that all will be well. Remember to trust God, and this too will pass.

Prayer Focus
BRAND NEW JOB SEEKER

Scripture: Isaiah 40:26

Write the scripture: read it aloud.

Praise: Focus on one attribute of God and give Him Praise:

Confession: Tell a forgiving God about your sins and ask for His forgiveness.

Petition: Make your specific request known to God .

Thanksgiving: Give thanks after making your petition; the blessing is on the way. Praise God for the blessing you anticipate.

In Jesus' Name, Amen.

Write your own personal Prayer

Reflection: How has God blessed you before?

Testimony: How has God exceeded your expectations in the past?

SEEKING GOD...EVEN MORE

Read the prayer from the book again; then read the prayer you've written. As you consider the prayers and listen for God's divine help in your job search, what action can you take this week, based on what you are hearing from God?

PLAN YOUR CONVERSATION WITH GOD.

Create an environment for prayer and reflection...where will you pray... what will you surround yourself with?

Will you listen to music to get into his presence? Or will there be total silence?

Commit to a specific time in the morning or in the evening to connect with God for five minutes..

PLAN TO ACT AFTER HEARING FROM GOD.

Decide who you will connect to for help related to your job search; include former coworkers, friends, mentors and organizations you belong to. Write down the contact information and follow through.

Who? _____

Contact Info? _____

How? _____

When? _____

Results of Contact: _____

_____

_____

You are taking a step closer to your dream job.

Prayer Focus
FREELANCER

Scripture: Psalm 90:17

Write the scripture:read it aloud.

Praise: Focus on one attribute of God and give Him Praise:

Confession: Tell a forgiving God about your sins and ask for His forgiveness.

Petition: Make your specific request known to God .

Thanksgiving: Give thanks after making your petition; the blessing is on the way. Praise God for the blessing you anticipate.

In Jesus' Name, Amen.

Write your own personal Prayer

Reflection: How has God blessed you before?

Testimony: How has God exceeded your expectations in the past?

SEEKING GOD...EVEN MORE

Read the prayer from the book again; then read the prayer you've written. As you consider the prayers and listen for God's divine help in your job search, what action can you take this week, based on what you are hearing from God?

PLAN YOUR CONVERSATION WITH GOD.

Create an environment for prayer and reflection...where will you pray... what will you surround yourself with?

Will you listen to music to get into his presence? Or will there be total silence?

Commit to a specific time in the morning or in the evening to connect with God for five minutes.

PLAN TO ACT AFTER HEARING FROM GOD.

Decide who you will connect to for help related to your job search; include former coworkers, friends, mentors and organizations you belong to. Write down the contact information and follow through.

Who? _____

Contact Info? _____

How? _____

When? _____

Results of Contact: _____

_____

_____

You are taking a step closer to your dream job.

Prayer Focus

THE FIRED JOB SEEKER

Scripture: Job 1:21

Write the scripture: read it aloud.

Praise: Focus on one attribute of God and give Him Praise:

Confession: Tell a forgiving God about your sins and ask for His forgiveness.

Petition: Make your specific request known to God .

Thanksgiving: Give thanks after making your petition; the blessing is on the way. Praise God for the blessing you anticipate.

In Jesus' Name, Amen.

Write your own personal Prayer

Write your own personal Prayer

Reflection: How has God blessed you before?

Testimony: How has God exceeded your expectations in the past?

SEEKING GOD...EVEN MORE

Read the prayer from the book again; then read the prayer you've written. As you consider the prayers and listen for God's divine help in your job search, what action can you take this week, based on what you are hearing from God?

PLAN YOUR CONVERSATION WITH GOD.

Create an environment for prayer and reflection...where will you pray... what will you surround yourself with?

Will you listen to music to get into his presence? Or will there be total silence?

Commit to a specific time in the morning or in the evening to connect with God for five minutes.

PLAN TO ACT AFTER HEARING FROM GOD.

Decide who you will connect to for help related to your job search; include former coworkers, friends, mentors and organizations you belong to. Write down the contact information and follow through.

Who? _____

Contact Info? _____

How? _____

When? _____

Results of Contact: _____

_____

_____

You are taking a step closer to your dream job.

Prayer Focus
LONG-TIME JOB SEEKER

Scripture: Isaiah 61:3

Write the scripture: read it aloud.

Praise: Focus on one attribute of God and give Him Praise:

Confession: Tell a forgiving God about your sins and ask for His forgiveness.

Petition: Make your specific request known to God .

Thanksgiving: Give thanks after making your petition; the blessing is on the way. Praise God for the blessing you anticipate.

In Jesus' Name, Amen.

Write your own personal Prayer

Write your own personal Prayer

Reflection: How has God blessed you before?

Testimony: How has God exceeded your expectations in the past?

SEEKING GOD...EVEN MORE

Read the prayer from the book again; then read the prayer you've written. As you consider the prayers and listen for God's divine help in your job search, what action can you take this week, based on what you are hearing from God?

PLAN YOUR CONVERSATION WITH GOD.

Create an environment for prayer and reflection...where will you pray... what will you surround yourself with?

Will you listen to music to get into his presence? Or will there be total silence?

Commit to a specific time in the morning or in the evening to connect with God for five minutes..

PLAN TO ACT AFTER HEARING FROM GOD.

Decide who you will connect to for help related to your job search; include former coworkers, friends, mentors and organizations you belong to. Write down the contact information and follow through.

Who? _____

Contact Info? _____

How? _____

When? _____

Results of Contact: _____

_____

_____

You are taking a step closer to your dream job.

Prayer Focus

TEMPORARY EMPLOYEE WHO WANTS FULL-TIME EMPLOYMENT

Scripture: Hebrews 11:1

Write the scripture: read it aloud.

Praise: Focus on one attribute of God and give Him Praise:

Confession: Tell a forgiving God about your sins and ask for His forgiveness.

Petition: Make your specific request known to God.

Thanksgiving: Give thanks after making your petition; the blessing is on the way. Praise God for the blessing you anticipate.

In Jesus' Name, Amen.

Write your own personal Prayer

Reflection: How has God blessed you before?

Testimony: How has God exceeded your expectations in the past?

SEEKING GOD...EVEN MORE

Read the prayer from the book again; then read the prayer you've written. As you consider the prayers and listen for God's divine help in your job search, what action can you take this week, based on what you are hearing from God?

PLAN YOUR CONVERSATION WITH GOD.

Create an environment for prayer and reflection...where will you pray... what will you surround yourself with?

Will you listen to music to get into his presence? Or will there be total silence?

Commit to a specific time in the morning or in the evening to connect with God for five minutes.

PLAN TO ACT AFTER HEARING FROM GOD.

Decide who you will connect to for help related to your job search; include former coworkers, friends, mentors and organizations you belong to. Write down the contact information and follow through.

Who? _____

Contact Info? _____

How? _____

When? _____

Results of Contact: _____

_____

_____

You are taking a step closer to your dream job.

Prayer Focus

JOB SEEKER WITH FINANCIAL PROBLEMS

Scripture: Luke 6:38

Write the scripture:read it aloud.

Praise: Focus on one attribute of God and give Him Praise:

Confession: Tell a forgiving God about your sins and ask for His forgiveness.

Petition: Make your specific request known to God .

Thanksgiving: Give thanks after making your petition; the blessing is on the way. Praise God for the blessing you anticipate.

In Jesus' Name, Amen.

Write your own personal Prayer

Reflection: How has God blessed you before?

Testimony: How has God exceeded your expectations in the past?

SEEKING GOD...EVEN MORE

Read the prayer from the book again; then read the prayer you've written. As you consider the prayers and listen for God's divine help in your job search, what action can you take this week, based on what you are hearing from God?

PLAN YOUR CONVERSATION WITH GOD.

Create an environment for prayer and reflection...where will you pray... what will you surround yourself with?

Will you listen to music to get into his presence? Or will there be total silence?

Commit to a specific time in the morning or in the evening to connect with God for five minutes.

PLAN TO ACT AFTER HEARING FROM GOD.

Decide who you will connect to for help related to your job search; include former coworkers, friends, mentors and organizations you belong to. Write down the contact information and follow through.

Who? _____

Contact Info? _____

How? _____

When? _____

Results of Contact: _____

_____

_____

You are taking a step closer to your dream job.

Prayer Focus
WHEN JOBS ARE SCARCE AND UNEMPLOYMENT HIGH

Scripture: 2 Corinthians 9:8

Write the scripture: read it aloud.

Praise: Focus on one attribute of God and give Him Praise:

Confession: Tell a forgiving God about your sins and ask for His forgiveness.

Petition: Make your specific request known to God .

Thanksgiving: Give thanks after making your petition; the blessing is on the way. Praise God for the blessing you anticipate.

In Jesus' Name, Amen.

Write your own personal Prayer

Reflection: How has God blessed you before?

Testimony: How has God exceeded your expectations in the past?

SEEKING GOD...EVEN MORE

Read the prayer from the book again; then read the prayer you've written. As you consider the prayers and listen for God's divine help in your job search, what action can you take this week, based on what you are hearing from God?

PLAN YOUR CONVERSATION WITH GOD.

Create an environment for prayer and reflection...where will you pray... what will you surround yourself with?

Will you listen to music to get into his presence? Or will there be total silence?

Commit to a specific time in the morning or in the evening to connect with God for five minutes.

PLAN TO ACT AFTER HEARING FROM GOD.

Decide who you will connect to for help related to your job search; include former coworkers, friends, mentors and organizations you belong to. Write down the contact information and follow through.

Who? _____

Contact Info? _____

How? _____

When? _____

Results of Contact: _____

_____

_____

You are taking a step closer to your dream job.

SECTION III
THE NEEDS OF THE JOB SEEKER

To find the right fit, you must know what you want. Imagine yourself in the perfect situation. You must know what you need for your breakthrough! Most job seekers think it is all about compensation. However, there are other aspects of the job that bring satisfaction. Don't be afraid to talk to God about all of your needs during your job search.

Prayer Focus

DECISION MAKING FOR JOB SEEKERS

Scripture: Daniel 2:21

Write the scripture:read it aloud.

Praise: Focus on one attribute of God and give Him Praise:

Confession: Tell a forgiving God about your sins and ask for His forgiveness.

Petition: Make your specific request known to God .

Thanksgiving: Give thanks after making your petition; the blessing is on the way. Praise God for the blessing you anticipate.

In Jesus' Name, Amen.

Write your own personal Prayer

Reflection: How has God blessed you before?

Testimony: How has God exceeded your expectations in the past?

SEEKING GOD...EVEN MORE

Read the prayer from the book again; then read the prayer you've written. As you consider the prayers and listen for God's divine help in your job search, what action can you take this week, based on what you are hearing from God?

PLAN YOUR CONVERSATION WITH GOD.

Create an environment for prayer and reflection...where will you pray... what will you surround yourself with?

Will you listen to music to get into his presence? Or will there be total silence?

Commit to a specific time in the morning or in the evening to connect with God for five minutes.

PLAN TO ACT AFTER HEARING FROM GOD.

Decide who you will connect to for help related to your job search; include former coworkers, friends, mentors and organizations you belong to. Write down the contact information and follow through.

Who? _____

Contact Info? _____

How? _____

When? _____

Results of Contact: _____

_____

_____

You are taking a step closer to your dream job.

Prayer Focus

JOB SEEKER WANTING TO RELOCATE

Scripture: Genesis 12:1-3

Write the scripture:read it aloud.

Praise: Focus on one attribute of God and give Him Praise:

Confession: Tell a forgiving God about your sins and ask for His forgiveness.

Petition: Make your specific request known to God .

Thanksgiving: Give thanks after making your petition; the blessing is on the way. Praise God for the blessing you anticipate.

In Jesus' Name, Amen.

Write your own personal Prayer

Reflection: How has God blessed you before?

Testimony: How has God exceeded your expectations in the past?

SEEKING GOD...EVEN MORE

Read the prayer from the book again; then read the prayer you've written. As you consider the prayers and listen for God's divine help in your job search, what action can you take this week, based on what you are hearing from God?

PLAN YOUR CONVERSATION WITH GOD.

Create an environment for prayer and reflection...where will you pray... what will you surround yourself with?

Will you listen to music to get into his presence? Or will there be total silence?

Commit to a specific time in the morning or in the evening to connect with God for five minutes.

PLAN TO ACT AFTER HEARING FROM GOD.

Decide who you will connect to for help related to your job search; include former coworkers, friends, mentors and organizations you belong to. Write down the contact information and follow through.

Who? _____

Contact Info? _____

How? _____

When? _____

Results of Contact: _____

_____

_____

You are taking a step closer to your dream job.

Prayer Focus

CHANGING CAREERS

Scripture: Psalm 71:6-7

Write the scripture: read it aloud.

Praise: Focus on one attribute of God and give Him Praise:

Confession: Tell a forgiving God about your sins and ask for His forgiveness.

Petition: Make your specific request known to God.

Thanksgiving: Give thanks after making your petition; the blessing is on the way. Praise God for the blessing you anticipate.

In Jesus' Name, Amen.

Write your own personal Prayer

Reflection: How has God blessed you before?

Testimony: How has God exceeded your expectations in the past?

SEEKING GOD...EVEN MORE

Read the prayer from the book again; then read the prayer you've written. As you consider the prayers and listen for God's divine help in your job search, what action can you take this week, based on what you are hearing from God?

PLAN YOUR CONVERSATION WITH GOD.

Create an environment for prayer and reflection...where will you pray... what will you surround yourself with?

Will you listen to music to get into his presence? Or will there be total silence?

Commit to a specific time in the morning or in the evening to connect with God for five minutes.

PLAN TO ACT AFTER HEARING FROM GOD.

Decide who you will connect to for help related to your job search; include former coworkers, friends, mentors and organizations you belong to. Write down the contact information and follow through.

Who? _____

Contact Info? _____

How? _____

When? _____

Results of Contact: _____

_____

_____

You are taking a step closer to your dream job.

Prayer Focus
JOB SEEKER WORKING REMOTELY

Scripture: Psalm 37:4

Write the scripture:read it aloud.

Praise: Focus on one attribute of God and give Him Praise:

Confession: Tell a forgiving God about your sins and ask for His forgiveness.

Petition: Make your specific request known to God .

Thanksgiving: Give thanks after making your petition; the blessing is on the way. Praise God for the blessing you anticipate.

In Jesus' Name, Amen.

Write your own personal Prayer

Reflection: How has God blessed you before?

Testimony: How has God exceeded your expectations in the past?

SEEKING GOD...EVEN MORE

Read the prayer from the book again; then read the prayer you've written. As you consider the prayers and listen for God's divine help in your job search, what action can you take this week, based on what you are hearing from God?

PLAN YOUR CONVERSATION WITH GOD.

Create an environment for prayer and reflection...where will you pray... what will you surround yourself with?

Will you listen to music to get into his presence? Or will there be total silence?

Commit to a specific time in the morning or in the evening to connect with God for five minutes.

PLAN TO ACT AFTER HEARING FROM GOD.

Decide who you will connect to for help related to your job search; include former coworkers, friends, mentors and organizations you belong to. Write down the contact information and follow through.

Who? _____

Contact Info? _____

How? _____

When? _____

Results of Contact: _____

_____

_____

You are taking a step closer to your dream job.

Prayer Focus

NEEDING A BREAKTHROUGH

Scripture: Lamentations 3:21-26

Write the scripture: read it aloud.

Praise: Focus on one attribute of God and give Him Praise:

Confession: Tell a forgiving God about your sins and ask for His forgiveness.

Petition: Make your specific request known to God .

Thanksgiving: Give thanks after making your petition; the blessing is on the way. Praise God for the blessing you anticipate.

In Jesus' Name, Amen.

Write your own personal Prayer

Reflection: How has God blessed you before?

Testimony: How has God exceeded your expectations in the past?

SEEKING GOD...EVEN MORE

Read the prayer from the book again; then read the prayer you've written. As you consider the prayers and listen for God's divine help in your job search, what action can you take this week, based on what you are hearing from God?

PLAN YOUR CONVERSATION WITH GOD.

Create an environment for prayer and reflection...where will you pray... what will you surround yourself with?

Will you listen to music to get into his presence? Or will there be total silence?

Commit to a specific time in the morning or in the evening to connect with God for five minutes.

PLAN TO ACT AFTER HEARING FROM GOD.

Decide who you will connect to for help related to your job search; include former coworkers, friends, mentors and organizations you belong to. Write down the contact information and follow through.

Who? _____

Contact Info? _____

How? _____

When? _____

Results of Contact: _____

_____

_____

You are taking a step closer to your dream job.

SECTION IV
THE JOB SEARCH PROCESS

One key to job search success is understanding the process. Most job seekers are not aware that an important key to an effective search is relationships with people. The first step is to master networking. However, the ultimate connection is God Almighty. Talking with Him makes seeking a job exponentially more effective than without prayer. God knows everyone. Knowing Him is a job search secret most people have not recognized as a factor in getting the job.

The remaining steps include:
- *Resume*
- *Interview*
- *Job Offer*
- *Accepting the Position*
- *Walking in Excellence*

Prayer Focus
JOB SEEKER WHO NEEDS CONNECTIONS

Scripture: John 15:7

Write the scripture: read it aloud.

Praise: Focus on one attribute of God and give Him Praise:

Confession: Tell a forgiving God about your sins and ask for His forgiveness.

Petition: Make your specific request known to God.

Thanksgiving: Give thanks after making your petition; the blessing is on the way. Praise God for the blessing you anticipate.

In Jesus' Name, Amen.

Write your own personal Prayer

Reflection: How has God blessed you before?

Testimony: How has God exceeded your expectations in the past?

SEEKING GOD...EVEN MORE

Read the prayer from the book again; then read the prayer you've written. As you consider the prayers and listen for God's divine help in your job search, what action can you take this week, based on what you are hearing from God?

PLAN YOUR CONVERSATION WITH GOD.

Create an environment for prayer and reflection...where will you pray... what will you surround yourself with?

Will you listen to music to get into his presence? Or will there be total silence?

Commit to a specific time in the morning or in the evening to connect with God for five minutes.

PLAN TO ACT AFTER HEARING FROM GOD.

Decide who you will connect to for help related to your job search; include former coworkers, friends, mentors and organizations you belong to. Write down the contact information and follow through.

Who? _____

Contact Info? _____

How? _____

When? _____

Results of Contact: _____

_____

_____

You are taking a step closer to your dream job.

Prayer Focus

JOB SEEKER'S RESUME

Scripture: Proverbs 3:3

Write the scripture: read it aloud.

Praise: Focus on one attribute of God and give Him Praise:

Confession: Tell a forgiving God about your sins and ask for His forgiveness.

Petition: Make your specific request known to God .

Thanksgiving: Give thanks after making your petition; the blessing is on the way. Praise God for the blessing you anticipate.

In Jesus' Name, Amen.

Write your own personal Prayer

Reflection: How has God blessed you before?

Testimony: How has God exceeded your expectations in the past?

SEEKING GOD...EVEN MORE

Read the prayer from the book again; then read the prayer you've written. As you consider the prayers and listen for God's divine help in your job search, what action can you take this week, based on what you are hearing from God?

PLAN YOUR CONVERSATION WITH GOD.

Create an environment for prayer and reflection...where will you pray... what will you surround yourself with?

Will you listen to music to get into his presence? Or will there be total silence?

Commit to a specific time in the morning or in the evening to connect with God for five minutes.

PLAN TO ACT AFTER HEARING FROM GOD.

Decide who you will connect to for help related to your job search; include former coworkers, friends, mentors and organizations you belong to. Write down the contact information and follow through.

Who? _____

Contact Info? _____

How? _____

When? _____

Results of Contact: _____

_____

_____

You are taking a step closer to your dream job.

Prayer Focus
PREPARING FOR THE INTERVIEW

Scripture: Proverbs 12:8

Write the scripture: read it aloud.

Praise: Focus on one attribute of God and give Him Praise:

Confession: Tell a forgiving God about your sins and ask for His forgiveness.

Petition: Make your specific request known to God .

Thanksgiving: Give thanks after making your petition; the blessing is on the way. Praise God for the blessing you anticipate.

In Jesus' Name, Amen.

Write your own personal Prayer

Reflection: How has God blessed you before?

Testimony: How has God exceeded your expectations in the past?

SEEKING GOD...EVEN MORE

Read the prayer from the book again; then read the prayer you've written. As you consider the prayers and listen for God's divine help in your job search, what action can you take this week, based on what you are hearing from God?

PLAN YOUR CONVERSATION WITH GOD.

Create an environment for prayer and reflection...where will you pray... what will you surround yourself with?

Will you listen to music to get into his presence? Or will there be total silence?

Commit to a specific time in the morning or in the evening to connect with God for five minutes.

PLAN TO ACT AFTER HEARING FROM GOD.

Decide who you will connect to for help related to your job search; include former coworkers, friends, mentors and organizations you belong to. Write down the contact information and follow through.

Who? _____

Contact Info? _____

How? _____

When? _____

Results of Contact: _____

_____

_____

You are taking a step closer to your dream job.

Prayer Focus
JOB OFFER

Scripture: Psalm 27:14

Write the scripture: read it aloud.

Praise: Focus on one attribute of God and give Him Praise:

Confession: Tell a forgiving God about your sins and ask for His forgiveness.

Petition: Make your specific request known to God .

Thanksgiving: Give thanks after making your petition; the blessing is on the way. Praise God for the blessing you anticipate.

In Jesus' Name, Amen.

Write your own personal Prayer

Reflection: How has God blessed you before?

Testimony: How has God exceeded your expectations in the past?

SEEKING GOD...EVEN MORE

Read the prayer from the book again; then read the prayer you've written. As you consider the prayers and listen for God's divine guidance. What action can you take this week to help you jump start a successful career in your new role?

PLAN YOUR CONVERSATION WITH GOD.

Create an environment for prayer and reflection...where will you pray... what will you surround yourself with?

Will you listen to music to get into his presence? Or will there be total silence?

Commit to a specific time in the morning or in the evening to connect with God for five minutes.

PLAN TO ACT AFTER HEARING FROM GOD.

Decide who you will get advice from to have success in your first 90 days in your new role; include former coworkers, friends, mentors and organizations. Write down the contact information and follow through.

Who? _____

Contact Info? _____

How? _____

When? _____

Results of Contact: _____

_____

_____

Praise God! You accomplished your goal! Now it's time to be the best in your new role!

Prayer Focus
GIVING THANKS FOR THE JOB

Scripture: 1 Chronicles 16:34

Write the scripture: read it aloud.

Praise: Focus on one attribute of God and give Him Praise:

Confession: Tell a forgiving God about your sins and ask for His forgiveness.

Petition: Make your specific request known to God.

Thanksgiving: Give thanks after making your petition; the blessing is on the way. Praise God for the blessing you anticipate.

In Jesus' Name, Amen.

Write your own personal Prayer

Reflection: How has God blessed you before?

Testimony: How has God exceeded your expectations in the past?

SEEKING GOD...EVEN MORE

Read the prayer from the book again; then read the prayer you've written. As you consider the prayers and listen for God's divine guidance. What action can you take this week to help you jump start a successful career in your new role?

PLAN YOUR CONVERSATION WITH GOD.

Create an environment for prayer and reflection...where will you pray... what will you surround yourself with?

Will you listen to music to get into his presence? Or will there be total silence?

Commit to a specific time in the morning or in the evening to connect with God for five minutes.

PLAN TO ACT AFTER HEARING FROM GOD.

Decide what internal organization and initiatives to participate in. Plan a strategy to have success in your first 90 days in your new role. Find internal contacts that can be a resource in helping you get acclimated to your position. Write down the contact information and follow through.

Who? _____

Contact Info? _____

How? _____

When? _____

Results of Contact: _____

_____

_____

You are taking a step closer to your dream job.

Prayer Focus

JOB SEEKER WHO DESIRES TO WALK IN EXCELLENCE

Scripture: Psalm 150:2

Write the scripture: read it aloud.

Praise: Focus on one attribute of God and give Him Praise:

Confession: Tell a forgiving God about your sins and ask for His forgiveness.

Petition: Make your specific request known to God.

Thanksgiving: Give thanks after making your petition; the blessing is on the way. Praise God for the blessing you anticipate.

In Jesus' Name, Amen.

Write your own personal Prayer

Reflection: How has God blessed you before?

Testimony: How has God exceeded your expectations in the past?

SEEKING GOD...EVEN MORE

Read the prayer from the book again; then read the prayer you've written. As you consider the prayers and listen for God's divine guidance. What action can you take this week to help you jump start a successful career in your new role?

PLAN YOUR CONVERSATION WITH GOD.

Create an environment for prayer and reflection...where will you pray... what will you surround yourself with?

Will you listen to music to get into his presence? Or will there be total silence?

Commit to a specific time in the morning or in the evening to connect with God for five minutes.

PLAN TO ACT AFTER HEARING FROM GOD.

Decide what internal organization and initiatives to participate in. Plan a strategy to have success in your first 90 days in your new role. Find internal contacts that can be a resource in helping you get acclimated to your position. Write down the contact information and follow through.

Who? _____

Contact Info? _____

How? _____

When? _____

Results of Contact: _____

_____

_____

You are taking a step closer to your dream job.

Affirmations

PLACE YOUR HAND ON YOUR HEART AND READ THE FOLLOWING ALOUD:

I will not fear because I have God's Word, His presence, and His Spirit on my side.

I rebuke anxiety when I focus on the Word of God.

I believe that the Greater One lives inside of me and increases my worth.

When I pray, I receive the joy of the Lord.

Just like His promises are new every morning, I am expecting God to do a new thing in my career.

I am free like the sea and I lean on God to navigate my path.

I cried to God and He heard my prayer.

My time is in the hands of the Lord.

I will be planted in a career where God leads me.

I depend on God's provision and not what is supplied by man.

The Federal Reserve controls the US economy and my personal economy is controlled by God.

I include God in every decision I make about my career.

Just like the birds, my career path is navigated by God.

Like the tide, the God of the Universe determines my direction.

I exceed expectations regardless of my location.

I server the God who originated the breakthrough.

I am prompted by God on making connections.

I have a resume that floats to the top.

I have witty words and my ideas solve problems In the workplace.

I choose the road to success.

I give thanks and leap for joy because God has blessed me with a new job.

I am a person of excellence.

PLACE YOUR HAND ON YOUR FOREHEAD AND READ THE FOLLOWING ALOUD.

[Say your name here] has the mind of Christ and the genius of Christ according to 1 Corinthians 2:16.

[Say your name here] is the head, not the tail. I will always be at the top, never at the bottom according to Deuteronomy 28:13.

[Say your name here] is strong in the Lord and in His mighty power according to Ephesians 6:10.

"You gain strength, courage and confidence by every experience in which you really stop to look fear in the face; You must do the thing you think you cannot do."

ELEANOR ROOSEVELT

JOB SEARCH ORGANIZER

It is a good idea to stay organized during your job search. Knowing and remembering names, places and people can be challenging if you have not recorded them along the way. This simple form will help you keep things in order. Having an organized record of your job search can also help with filing for unemployment benefits. Being organized is a factor in having a spirit of excellence.

Organization Name:	
Date Applied:	
Position(s) Applied for:	
Initial Contact Person:	
Position Type Full-Time ☐ Part-Time ☐ Contract-to-Hire ☐	

Networking Connections	
Name	
Email	
Phone	Method of Contact
Date of First Contact	
Date of Second Contact	

GOD, PLEASE HELP ME FIND A JOB

HR Professional	
Name	
Email	
Phone	Method of Contact

Hiring Manager	
Department Name	
Name	
Email	
Phone	Method of Contact

☐ Resume Sent Resume Filename	☐ Cover Letter Sent Cover Letter Filename

☐ Background check done	Date of drug test

Interview #1
Date / Time
Interview Format
(Zoom, Video, Phone, On-Site, Panel)
Contact Person
Thank You Sent
Outcome
Feedback

Interview #2
Date / Time
Interview Format
(Zoom, Video, Phone, On-Site, Panel)
Contact Person
Thank You Sent
Outcome
Feedback

Interview #3
Date / Time
Interview Format
(Zoom, Video, Phone, On-Site, Panel)
Contact Person
Thank You Sent
Outcome
Feedback

Salary Mentioned
Salary Range
Key Benefits
Pros of this Job:
Cons of this Job:

Notes:

Organization Name:
Date Applied:
Position(s) Applied for:
Initial Contact Person:
Position Type Full-Time ☐ Part-Time ☐ Contract-to-Hire ☐

Networking Connections	
Name	
Email	
Phone	Method of Contact
Date of First Contact	
Date of Second Contact	

HR Professional	
Name	
Email	
Phone	Method of Contact

Hiring Manager	
Department Name	
Name	
Email	
Phone	Method of Contact

☐ Resume Sent Resume Filename	☐ Cover Letter Sent Cover Letter Filename

☐ Background check done	Date of drug test

Interview #1
Date / Time
Interview Format
(Zoom, Video, Phone, On-Site, Panel)
Contact Person
Thank You Sent
Outcome
Feedback

Interview #2

Date / Time
Interview Format
(Zoom, Video, Phone, On-Site, Panel)
Contact Person
Thank You Sent
Outcome
Feedback

Interview #3
Date / Time
Interview Format
(Zoom, Video, Phone, On-Site, Panel)
Contact Person
Thank You Sent
Outcome
Feedback

Salary Mentioned	
Salary Range	
Key Benefits	
Pros of this Job:	
Cons of this Job:	

Notes:

Organization Name:
Date Applied:
Position(s) Applied for:
Initial Contact Person:
Position Type Full-Time ☐ Part-Time ☐ Contract-to-Hire ☐

Networking Connections	
Name	
Email	
Phone	Method of Contact
Date of First Contact	
Date of Second Contact	

HR Professional	
Name	
Email	
Phone	Method of Contact

Hiring Manager	
Department Name	
Name	
Email	
Phone	Method of Contact

☐ Resume Sent Resume Filename	☐ Cover Letter Sent Cover Letter Filename

☐ Background check done	Date of drug test

Interview #1
Date / Time
Interview Format
(Zoom, Video, Phone, On-Site, Panel)
Contact Person
Thank You Sent
Outcome
Feedback

Interview #2	
Date / Time	
Interview Format	
(Zoom, Video, Phone, On-Site, Panel)	
Contact Person	
Thank You Sent	
Outcome	
Feedback	

Interview #3
Date / Time
Interview Format
(Zoom, Video, Phone, On-Site, Panel)
Contact Person
Thank You Sent
Outcome
Feedback

Salary Mentioned
Salary Range
Key Benefits
Pros of this Job:
Cons of this Job:

Notes:

Organization Name:	
Date Applied:	
Position(s) Applied for:	
Initial Contact Person:	
Position Type Full-Time ☐ Part-Time ☐ Contract-to-Hire ☐	

Networking Connections	
Name	
Email	
Phone	Method of Contact
Date of First Contact	
Date of Second Contact	

HR Professional	
Name	
Email	
Phone	Method of Contact

Hiring Manager	
Department Name	
Name	
Email	
Phone	Method of Contact

☐ Resume Sent Resume Filename	☐ Cover Letter Sent Cover Letter Filename

☐ Background check done	Date of drug test

Interview #1
Date / Time
Interview Format
(Zoom, Video, Phone, On-Site, Panel)
Contact Person
Thank You Sent
Outcome
Feedback

Interview #2

Date / Time
Interview Format
(Zoom, Video, Phone, On-Site, Panel)
Contact Person
Thank You Sent
Outcome
Feedback

Interview #3
Date / Time
Interview Format
(Zoom, Video, Phone, On-Site, Panel)
Contact Person
Thank You Sent
Outcome
Feedback

Salary Mentioned
Salary Range
Key Benefits
Pros of this Job:
Cons of this Job:

Notes:

Organization Name:
Date Applied:
Position(s) Applied for:
Initial Contact Person:
Position Type Full-Time ☐ Part-Time ☐ Contract-to-Hire ☐

Networking Connections	
Name	
Email	
Phone	Method of Contact
Date of First Contact	
Date of Second Contact	

HR Professional	
Name	
Email	
Phone	Method of Contact

Hiring Manager	
Department Name	
Name	
Email	
Phone	Method of Contact

☐ Resume Sent Resume Filename	☐ Cover Letter Sent Cover Letter Filename

☐ Background check done	Date of drug test

Interview #1
Date / Time
Interview Format
(Zoom, Video, Phone, On-Site, Panel)
Contact Person
Thank You Sent
Outcome
Feedback

Interview #2
Date / Time
Interview Format
(Zoom, Video, Phone, On-Site, Panel)
Contact Person
Thank You Sent
Outcome
Feedback

Interview #3	
Date / Time	
Interview Format	
(Zoom, Video, Phone, On-Site, Panel)	
Contact Person	
Thank You Sent	
Outcome	
Feedback	

Salary Mentioned	
Salary Range	
Key Benefits	
Pros of this Job:	
Cons of this Job:	

Notes:

Organization Name:
Date Applied:
Position(s) Applied for:
Initial Contact Person:
Position Type Full-Time ☐ Part-Time ☐ Contract-to-Hire ☐

Networking Connections	
Name	
Email	
Phone	Method of Contact
Date of First Contact	
Date of Second Contact	

HR Professional	
Name	
Email	
Phone	Method of Contact

Hiring Manager	
Department Name	
Name	
Email	
Phone	Method of Contact

☐ Resume Sent Resume Filename	☐ Cover Letter Sent Cover Letter Filename

☐ Background check done	Date of drug test

Interview #1
Date / Time
Interview Format
(Zoom, Video, Phone, On-Site, Panel)
Contact Person
Thank You Sent
Outcome
Feedback

Interview #2

Date / Time
Interview Format
(Zoom, Video, Phone, On-Site, Panel)
Contact Person
Thank You Sent
Outcome
Feedback

Interview #3
Date / Time
Interview Format
(Zoom, Video, Phone, On-Site, Panel)
Contact Person
Thank You Sent
Outcome
Feedback

Salary Mentioned
Salary Range
Key Benefits
Pros of this Job:
Cons of this Job:

Notes:

Organization Name:
Date Applied:
Position(s) Applied for:
Initial Contact Person:
Position Type Full-Time ☐ Part-Time ☐ Contract-to-Hire ☐

Networking Connections	
Name	
Email	
Phone	Method of Contact
Date of First Contact	
Date of Second Contact	

HR Professional	
Name	
Email	
Phone	Method of Contact

Hiring Manager	
Department Name	
Name	
Email	
Phone	Method of Contact

☐ Resume Sent Resume Filename	☐ Cover Letter Sent Cover Letter Filename

☐ Background check done	Date of drug test

Interview #1
Date / Time
Interview Format
(Zoom, Video, Phone, On-Site, Panel)
Contact Person
Thank You Sent
Outcome
Feedback

Interview #2
Date / Time
Interview Format
(Zoom, Video, Phone, On-Site, Panel)
Contact Person
Thank You Sent
Outcome
Feedback

Interview #3
Date / Time
Interview Format
(Zoom, Video, Phone, On-Site, Panel)
Contact Person
Thank You Sent
Outcome
Feedback

Salary Mentioned
Salary Range
Key Benefits
Pros of this Job:
Cons of this Job:

Notes:

It's Not Over

Thanks for praying these prayers and for taking a time to reflect and write your own. If you would like to continue on this encouragement path, please connect with me. You can receive support for your job hunt journey and engage with me on my website: https://blessthework.com. My email address is blessthework@gmail.com.

Receive a FREE download with practical job search tips you can implement to enhance your search.

Also, if you have enjoyed these books, leave a positive review on https://amazon.com.

About the Author

Sonia H. Cameron is a blogger who writes to encourage working people. She has written "Prayers for Your Career" as part of the https://blessthework.com website since 2010. On June 17, 2014, her first devotional article for Christian Devotions was published.

Sonia began her career in the corporate world as an intern with a local utility firm. She has had career ups and downs, and she loves to share them. Sonia is currently a technical support engineer with a corporation in Research Triangle Park, NC. She is married and has a blended family with wonderful children. Sonia loves to cook, and she also cooks to love.

You may contact Sonia via email at sonia@blessthework.com or via the website https://blessthework.com

www.ingramcontent.com/pod-product-compliance

Lightning Source LLC
Chambersburg PA
CBHW071343080526
4458 7CB000 17B/2944